Vocal/Piano

Billie Holiday
ORIGINAL KEYS FOR SINGERS

Transcribed by John Nicholas

Photo courtesy of Institute of Jazz Studies

ISBN 0-634-02587-2

HAL•LEONARD®
CORPORATION

7777 W. BLUEMOUND RD. P.O. BOX 13819 MILWAUKEE, WI 53213

Visit Hal Leonard Online at
www.halleonard.com

Billie Holiday

ORIGINAL KEYS FOR SINGERS

CONTENTS

Biography

She is one of the most beloved singers in American history, praised by such artists as Tony Bennett, Frank Sinatra, Benny Goodman, Rosemary Clooney, Sylvia Sims, and Judy Garland. While her records were never huge sellers in their day, most of them have remained in print ever since they were first issued. She is continually discovered and rediscovered by new generations of fans, musicians and singers, and some of her recordings are among the finest vocal performances ever made.

Billie Holiday was born Eleanora Harris in Baltimore on April 7, 1915. Her parents were teenagers; there is no evidence that they ever married. Her father, Clarence Holiday, a professional guitarist, abandoned mother and child, and didn't acknowledge Billie as his daughter until she became successful.

Life for Eleanora was difficult from the start. She was raped by a neighbor at the age of ten, was packed off to live with Baltimore relatives when her mother moved to New York, and soon after was sent to a home for wayward girls. In 1927, Eleanora joined mother Sadie in Brooklyn, where mother worked as a domestic and daughter (now nicknamed Billie because her mother loved the screen actress Billie Dove) also found domestic work, albeit at a Harlem brothel. Billie was briefly jailed for prostitution. The owner loved jazz, and Billie heard her first Louis Armstrong and Bessie Smith records while working there. Billie later said she learned to sing by imitating "Pops." In 1946, she would act and sing with Armstrong in a movie called *New Orleans*.

By her late teens Billie was singing in Harlem clubs, where talent scout and producer John Hammond heard her. Hammond was immediately taken with Holiday's sound and phrasing, and told everyone in his circle of this new singer who sounded like no one he'd ever heard. He arranged for Holiday to make her first recordings in November of 1933 with a small group led by Benny Goodman. Hammond later hired her to sing on a series of recordings led by pianist Teddy Wilson for Brunswick. Holiday also made recordings under her own name for the cheaper-priced Vocalion label. While many of the songs were pop fodder, Holiday's vocalizing turned them into prized classics, and they were on hundreds of jukeboxes across the country.

Hammond also put Billie together with Count Basie, another artist he discovered and promoted. Holiday toured with the Basie band during 1937, but could not record with it since she and Count were signed to different record labels. Holiday later joined the Artie Shaw orchestra, one of the first black musicians to tour with a white ensemble. It was a daring move in the late 1930s, and Billie did not last long on the tour, although she had nothing but good things to say about Shaw in later life. She returned to New York club work and recording. A breakthrough was being booked into a Greenwich Village nightclub that played to a sophisticated audience.

One day Billie heard a song dealing with racism in the South. She immediately wanted to record it, but was turned down by Columbia, the company that bought Brunswick and Vocalion. She complained to Milt Gabler, owner of the Commodore Record Shop on 42nd Street in New York City. Gabler owned his own record label, and got permission to record Holiday singing "Strange Fruit." The song was immediately banned in Great Britain and many radio stations in the United States refused to play it, but it became a cult hit and was requested repeatedly by Holiday fans, ultimately to her dismay and annoyance.

Gabler later became a producer at Decca Records, and one of the first things he did was to offer Billie a contract. Upon signing with the label, Holiday requested that a string section be added to her accompaniments. Strings were a rare luxury for jazz sessions of any type, but Gabler agreed, believing that such accompaniment would get Billie's records the same attention as recordings by Perry Como, Frank Sinatra, and Dinah Shore. Such recordings as "Lover Man," "No More," "That Ole Devil Called Love," and "Good Morning Heartache" date from this period. Most historians agree that her five years with Decca (1944-49) were her strongest vocally. She achieved national fame in the years after World War II.

Unfortunately, Holiday's drug addiction and her stormy relationships and marriages took their toll on the singer's voice and personal life. She spent most of the year 1947 in jail. When she was released, she was unable to sing in New York clubs due to the loss of her cabaret license, but she toured extensively, her fame boosted by calamity. Impresario Norman Granz added her to his "Jazz at the Philharmonic" tour packages, and recorded her for his Clef and Verve labels during the 1950s. Her voice continued to deteriorate, but performances such as the 1956 Carnegie Hall "comeback" concert were well-publicized and major musical events. She wrote her autobiography, *Lady Sings the Blues*, with the help of ghostwriter Bill Dufty. While it brought her a burst of celebrity, those who knew the real story of Billie Holiday knew the book to be mostly fiction. (The film based on the book, starring Diana Ross, Billy Dee Williams and Richard Pryor, was even more fictionalized; staunch Holiday fans were outraged by the movie.)

On May 31, 1959 Holiday collapsed in her New York apartment and was brought to Metropolitan Hospital. Police found heroin in her sick room and she was placed under arrest even when severely ill. She never recovered, and died on July 17, 1959. Holiday left an enormous legacy of hundreds of studio and live performances of rare artistry. Her performances continue to inspire singers of all types of music. Along with Louis Armstrong, Ella Fitzgerald and Sarah Vaughn, Billie Holiday defined 20th century vocal jazz for all time.

Discography

Except for "You've Changed," all of the recordings transcribed in this book were originally issued as 78 RPM single records. The original release number is included in the listing below. During the 1980s, Columbia issued nine individual CDs and one boxed set of the Billie Holiday recordings owned by that label at that time. In October of 2001, Columbia released a 10 CD complete Billie Holiday set of all of her recordings for the Brunswick, Vocalion, and Okeh labels from 1933-44. This set is highly recommended for its much-improved sound quality, its extensive notes, and its packaging. The catalog number is CXK 85470.

Similarly, all of Billie's Commodore and Decca recordings are available in complete boxed sets. The Commodore sides are on Verve, and the Decca sides are on GRP.

Recordings on the Brunswick label were led by Teddy Wilson, and were released under his name. Vocalion and Okeh were issued as Billie Holiday and Her Orchestra. Where available, arranger credits are given.

All of Me (3/21/41) – OK 6214
Billie's Blues (I Love My Man) (4/8/44) – Commodore CMS 614
Body and Soul (2/29/40) – Vocalion 5481
Crazy He Calls Me (10/19/49 – Arr. and Cond. By Gordon Jenkins) – Decca 24796
Easy Living (6/1/37) – Brunswick 7911
Fine and Mellow (4/20/39) – Commodore CMS 526
A Fine Romance (7/2/35) – Brunswick 7501
God Bless' the Child (5/9/41) – OK 6270
Good Morning Heartache (1/22/46) – Decca 23676
I Cried for You (7/30/36) – Brunswick 7729
I Wished on the Moon (7/2/35) – Brunswick 7501
Lover, Come Back to Me (4/8/44) – Commodore CMS 559
Miss Brown to You (7/2/35) – Brunswick 7501
Solitude (2/13/47 – Arr. and Cond. by Bob Haggart) – Decca 23853
Some Other Spring (7/5/39) – Vocalion 5021
Strange Fruit (4/20/39) – Commodore CMS 526
This Year's Kisses (1/25/37) – Brunswick 7789
The Very Thought of You (9/15/38) – Vocalion 4457
You've Changed (2/20/58 – Arr. and Cond. by Ray Ellis) – Columbia CS 8048; CD: Columbia

Billie Holiday

ORIGINAL KEYS FOR SINGERS

Transcribed from Historic Recordings

ALL OF ME

Words and Music by SEYMOUR SIMONS
and GERALD MARKS

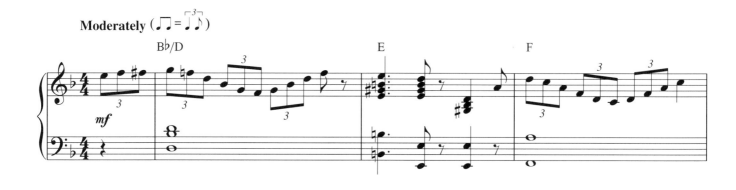

All of me, _____ why _ not take _

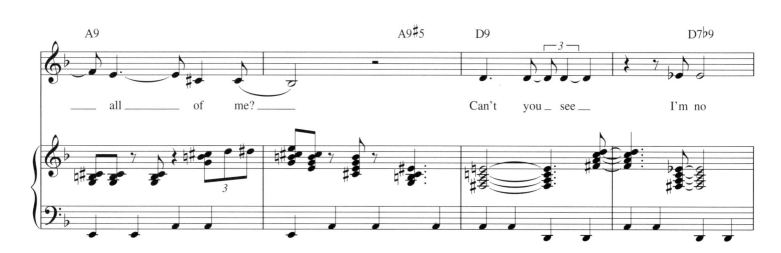

_ all _____ of _ me? _____ Can't you _ see _ I'm no

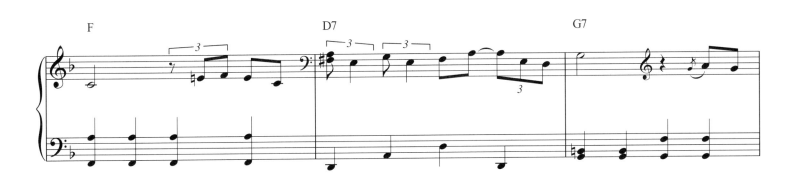

Ba - by, _____ take all of _____ me. _____

BILLIE'S BLUES
(I Love My Man)

Words and Music by
BILLIE HOLIDAY

BODY AND SOUL

Words by EDWARD HEYMAN,
ROBERT SOUR and FRANK EYTON
Music by JOHN GREEN

CRAZY HE CALLS ME

Words and Music by BOB RUSSELL
and CARL SIGMAN

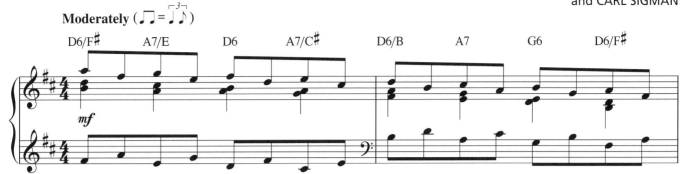

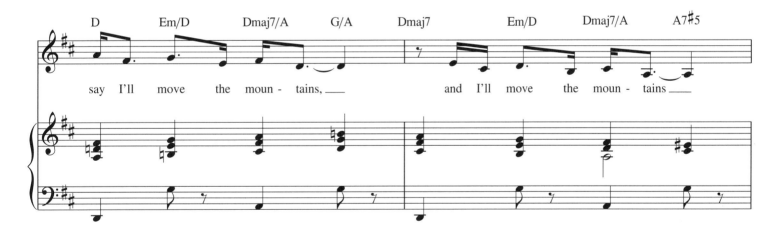

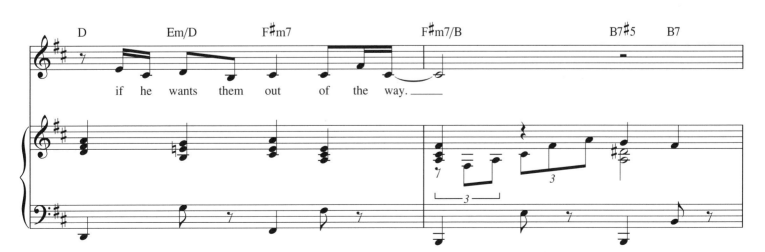

EASY LIVING
Theme from the Paramount Picture EASY LIVING

Words and Music by LEO ROBIN
and RALPH RAINGER

FINE AND MELLOW

Words and Music by
BILLIE HOLIDAY

My man don't love me, treats me aw - ful mean.

My man, he don't love me, ___ treats me aw - ful mean. He's the

A FINE ROMANCE

Words by DOROTHY FIELDS
Music by JEROME KERN

Moderately Fast

fine _____ ro - mance _____   with   no   kiss -
fine _____ ro - mance _____   my   good   fel -

GOD BLESS' THE CHILD

Words and Music by ARTHUR HERZOG JR.
and BILLIE HOLIDAY

GOOD MORNING HEARTACHE

Words and Music by DAN FISHER,
IRENE HIGGINBOTHAM and ERVIN DRAKE

44

I CRIED FOR YOU

Words and Music by ARTHUR FREED,
GUS ARNHEIM and ABE LYMAN

I WISHED ON THE MOON

Words and Music by DOROTHY PARKER
and RALPH RAINGER

LOVER, COME BACK TO ME

Lyrics by OSCAR HAMMERSTEIN II
Music by SIGMUND ROMBERG

The sky was blue, and high a-bove. The moon was new, and so was love.
You came at last, love had it's day. That day is past, you've gone a-way.

MISS BROWN TO YOU

Words and Music by LEO ROBIN,
RICHARD A. WHITING and RALPH RAINGER

Just wait and you'll see the lov - a - ble, lit - tle Miss Brown _

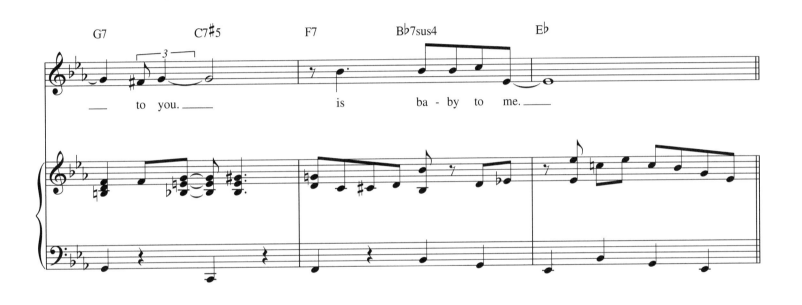

_ to you. _ is ba - by to me. _

SOLITUDE

Words and Music by DUKE ELLINGTON,
EDDIE De LANGE and IRVING MILLS

SOME OTHER SPRING

Words and Music by ARTHUR HERZOG, Jr.
and IRENE KITCHINGS

STRANGE FRUIT

Words and Music by
LEWIS ALLAN

THIS YEAR'S KISSES

from the 20th Century Fox Motion Picture ON THE AVENUE

Words and Music by
IRVING BERLIN

72

THE VERY THOUGHT OF YOU

Words and Music by
RAY NOBLE

To Coda

YOU'VE CHANGED

Words and Music by BILL CAREY
and CARL FISCHER